DAILY WISDOM

"That Still Small Voice"

James V. Daniels

All rights reserved. No part of this publication may be reproduced, stored in retrieval system, or transmitted in any form or by any means for example, electronic, photocopy, recording without the prior written permission of the author.

Unless otherwise indicated, all Scripture quotations are taken from The New King James Version of the Bible. Copyright © 1979, 1980, 1982, by Thomas Nelson, Inc., Publishers. Used by permission.

Scripture quotations marked NIV are taken from The Holy Bible, New International Version®, NIV® Copyright ©1973, 1978, 1984, by International

Bible Society ® Used by permission. All rights reserved worldwide.

Daily Wisdom

"That Still Small Voice"

Copyright © 2016

by James V Daniels

TABLE OF CONTENTS

INTRODUCTION

1. LIFE IS A BLESSING FROM GOD BE HAPPY

2. FOCUS ON THE POSITIVE

3. THEY'RE JUST ORDINARY PEOPLE

4. IS NICE BEING STUPID?

5. MY SECRET TO SUSTAINING PEACE

6. OVERCOMING ISSUES WITH FAMILY MEMBERS

7. COUNT YOUR BLESSINGS NOT YOUR PROBLEMS

8. LIVE YOUR LIFE LIKE THERE IS NO TOMORROW

9. SMILE AND LAUGH AS MUCH AS POSSIBLE

10. MIRACLES BRING JOY

11. DO YOU BELIEVE IN ANGELS?

12. LOVE LIKE JESUS LOVES

BOOK ACKNOWLEDGEMENTS

INTRODUCTION

I believe that every person in the world wants to be happy and have peace daily in life. Unfortunately, many people do not feel this happiness or peace. Either they don't know how to, or they are looking in the wrong places. I used to be one of those people and at times I must remind myself that is who I choose not to be. A very wise Pastor once said," First you dream it...then you believe it...then you live it!"

I choose to be happy and have peace and I attempt to live it each and everyday. Through my journey of five decades here on earth, I have learned through my life experiences, time, and wisdom while serving in the military and the postal service and most of all through the love of God, how to make myself happy and enjoy peace of mind. Most people don't know that being happy is a choice that we make for ourselves. It's how we deal with everyday life, how we let certain things affect us, how we let words affect us, how we let our situations affect us, and how others affect us.

Do I ever get angry? Yes. Am I perfect? No. Do I remain happy and keep my peace of mind? Yes. We all get angry sometimes, even God got angry. But if we don't use our anger for bad or to seek revenge or use it in an ungodly way it's ok. We are all human beings made in the image of God and we all sin and lose it every now and then, some more than others. Maintaining your peace and being happy feels like work sometimes, but it's ok. The end results are amazing when you succeed.

I was asked by a customer one day:" James, how are you able to stay happy and cheerful all the time? You're funny. You should write a book." Laughing, I said," Write a book? About what? The customer said," About the stuff you talk about. You should get a voice recorder and record yourself and write about that." A few days went by, and I saw that customer again and I said, "You really think I should write a book?" that person said absolutely, but still I had a question mark. What was my topic? A little more time passed before it came to me. I decided to write about the question that people ask me the most, and that is how I stay so happy, cheerful, and at peace all the time.

So, I would like to share with everyone my personal experiences of how I keep myself happy and at peace and how I came to this point in my life. And how I'm unwilling to give it up for any amount of money or for the things of the world.

Chapter 1

Life is a blessing from God be happy

As I start my day, and my feet hit the floor from my bed, I give thanks to God for another day of life here on earth. I pray this prayer every morning: "Dear God, thank you Jesus for waking me up this morning, thank you for another day here on earth, thank you for everything that you do, in Jesus' name I pray, Amen." Then I take about 5 to 10 minutes to wake up. Then I grab my Bible and grab my journal and go to a quiet place in my house, where it's just me and God.

Once I'm there I pray again: "Dear God, I ask you for the wisdom, knowledge, and understanding of your word, the ability to apply it to my life and your guidance to help me do so, in Jesus Name I pray, Amen." Then I open my Bible and I read where I left off from the day before. I always read three chapters. After I am done reading, I have a journal that I write in. It's like a diary. I pick out the scripture that stood out to me the most, then I write it in my journal. Then I write an observation of the scripture, meaning what the scripture was about in my own words. Then I write an application, meaning how am I going to use that scripture in my life to better myself in God's eyes. Lastly, after I'm finished, I pray to God to help me incorporate what I read into my life, and I write down the prayer that I prayed.

The time I spend with God in the morning is about 30 to 40 minutes which is nothing compared to all the meaningless things we humans do daily. I get up 45 minutes early so I can spend time with Him.

I try to read my Bible and journal in the morning because I want God first in my life. He is the reason I am alive. Secondly, I find that when I spend time with God in the morning, I'm happy and I have peace from the beginning of my day. I go to my job not dreading going there but thankful to have a job and wanting to do the best job that I can. I am reminded that God blessed me with this job and gave it to me and expects me to do a good job. So, I don't let the negatives of the job or the negatives of the people I encounter stop me. I do my best to keep a smile, be happy, cheerful, and at peace, even when I don't feel like it. *Yes, even when I don't feel like it.* I look at it this way: it's easier to be nice to someone and maintain your peace then get angry and upset and lose it. That's destroying your peace and throwing happy right out of the window.

I pay a price when I don't spend time in the mornings with God. If I start my day and start doing other things first, my days are a lot more challenging. Little things may irritate me, and my tolerance is a little short for the negatives of the job and the negatives of the people I encounter. But even if I miss my Bible / journaling time, I keep my peace. I accomplish this by talking to myself inside, saying: *shut up James, walk in love, it's just a test, it could be worse*. Even though I feel that still small voice from God inside talking to me, which I believe is the Holy Spirit. Putting those words in me to minister to myself. Listening to that voice keeps me at peace with myself until my day is over. After work, I find I'm happy once again. And when I look back on my day. I was able to have a positive impact on my work environment and a positive impact on the people I serve in the community.

The word happy is a gift of love from God. A gift of fun, a gift of giggles, no worries, feeling good about yourself. Having a smile as big as the sun. As I stated in my introduction, being happy is a choice that we all have. Some of the words just mentioned are feelings and emotions of a person being happy.

When I say we all have a choice to be happy, it's true because if you aren't happy, it's no one's fault except your own. It's what you let affect your emotions that cause you to be unhappy. Everyone has his or her own definition of what the word happy means to them. For me being honest, having integrity, moral values, being trustworthy are some of the things that make me happy. I don't have the worries of a dishonest person and it makes me feel good and gives me peace inside to know that I want to be righteous in this area of my life and righteous in the eyes of God.

Let me also put this out there: *we all have flaws*. There is no person on the planet that is 100% perfect or better than the rest of us. We all have our strengths and weaknesses in different areas of our lives. We must take the things that affect our happiness and peace of mind and turn them into a plus sign by using the gift of love that God put inside each and everyone of us. Which reminds me of one of my favorite passages in the Bible.

Love is patient, love is kind, it does not envy, it does not boast, it is not proud. It is not rude, it is not self-seeking, it is not easily angered, it keeps no record of wrongs. Love does not delight in evil but rejoices with the truth. It always protects, always trust, always hopes, always perseveres. (1 Corinthians 13:4-7 NIV)

Bottom line, if you want to be happy and have peace, you must work at it. Use the gift of love with which God has blessed us all. Remember being happy is a choice. You don't have to be 100% perfect to experience happiness and peace. Our Savor Jesus Christ is the only perfect one and he died for our sins that we may have the opportunity for eternal life in heaven with him.

At the same time, he wants us to be obedient here on earth and love one another and to be happy and have peace.

Chapter 2

Focus on the positive

Do you believe that a negative can be turned into a positive? Because if you do, you have just turned a negative into a positive.

When something happens that is out of our control, we tend to be sad, disappointed, a little mad, and believe it or not some of us become depressed because we are focusing on the negative instead of the positive. That's just human nature and that is how we are wired to think sometimes. We are also wired to be patient and think positive. Meaning look at the good in something instead of the bad.

When people say things like," that's really messed up, I have to work this holiday weekend," I wish I had a bigger car," I hate Monday mornings.' "My parents treat me like I'm a child."

These are all negative comments, but if we focus on the positive, we can eliminate a lot of these negative emotions in our lives. Just take "I have to work this holiday weekend" for instance. What do you see that is positive in this statement? Number one, you have a job and are not unemployed. Number two, you are probably getting paid time and a half because its a holiday weekend, you're going to be looking good at the bank next pay period. Three, you are saving money you would have blown the weekend had you been off work. Four, keep in mind it's just another day that man gave a name to celebrate. Lastly, it could be God almighty saving you from the unforeseen. We always hear these stories on the news: someone being delayed, which caused them not to get on that plane that just crashed. Or on that freeway where the bridge collapsed around the time, they would have been on it. Or some sports bar was raided by the cops that weekend where the person normally hangs out.

Don't give up when things don't go in your favor and cause you to be negative. Look at what is good in the situation, then focus on the positive. It will eliminate the disappointments and bad feelings. Don't listen to others that are always negative. Surround yourself with positive people.

Now let's look at the bigger picture regarding focusing on the positive.

Picture a collision. You were involved in an automobile accident. Your vehicle was totaled, and you had minor injuries. You're more concerned about the car because you no longer have transportation to work and what your spouse is going to say about the wrecked car.

That is clearly not focusing on the positive. If that person was clearly focusing on the positive, they would be thankful to be alive and that they were able to walk away from the accident. It could have been fatal. They shouldn't be worried about what their spouse is going to say about the car (you can replace a car not a life). I'm quite sure that spouse would rather have their mate, than a car. If not, I would say you probably married the wrong person.

When the unforeseen happens, we must be prepared to deal with the negative by focusing on the positive and being patient.

A negative appearance can be deceiving most of the time. Meaning things are not as bad as they appear to be at that moment. We need to let the dust settle, relax our minds, calm ourselves down from all the excitement of the disappointment, and look at the situation with a clear and positive mind. Focusing on the positive is kind of like deciding to be happy instead of feeling or speaking negativity into existence. In the Bible the book of James speaks about the power of the tongue how we can speak life into existence or speak death into existence in our everyday life.

But no man can tame the tongue. It is an unruly evil, full of deadly poison. With it we bless our God and Father, and with it we curse men, who have been made in the similitude of God. Out of the same mouth proceed blessing and cursing. My brethren, these things ought not to be so. (James 3:8-10)

The word cursing in James chapter three doesn't mean cursing like saying a bad word. It means we curse ourselves by what comes out of our mouths when it is negative. As I said previously you are speaking the negative into existence in your life. Where focusing on the positive you are speaking blessings into your lives.

We all need to focus on the positive, not only will it keep you happy, but it will also keep away the gray hairs before you are supposed to get them.

Chapter 3

They're just ordinary people

I used to get mad and upset with people sometimes, I thought how could someone be so rude and nasty towards another person? And, no, I'm not talking about the race card. I'm just talking about being rude towards another person because you can. So, I made up my mind that I wouldn't let this affect me.

I told myself I need to continue to be the person that God made me to be, which is friendly and kind to others. From that point on I just started speaking to people daily as I encountered them, whether on my job or in public. Just simply saying "hello", "good morning", "good afternoon", "have a nice day", or other greetings along those lines. I would do it with a smile and enthusiasm. Some people responded back with smiles, thank you's, and kind words, which made me feel good, happy, and joyful. I still got a few nonresponses, the rolling of the eyes, the grumbling, and the negative comments from some. For instance, I would say: "Good morning" or "have a nice day," they would respond back in a negative way like:" What's so good about the morning? and keep walking.

As time passed, I started to realize that I no longer cared about the negative comments that people made when I encountered them daily. It no longer affected me in a way where it was stealing my peace and my joy. I still spoke and remained kind to the people who were negative towards me when I saw them again. Believe it or not, when I saw some of them again, they stopped and said "Hey, I just want to apologize for the other day not speaking when you said, 'good morning.' My mind was elsewhere." or "Hey, I'm sorry. I was going through something that day." That's also when I learned that we shouldn't get upset or mad because someone didn't respond back to our kindness or niceness. You never know what's going on in a person's mind or life at that moment. So, don't let it affect you. Continue to walk in love and say to yourself that this person may be having a bad day and not let it steal your joy and peace.

We are all just ordinary people, and when I say this a sweet little old lady comes to mind. But at the time she was the opposite of sweet. And I must tell this story, true story I may add. I used to walk past this little old lady on my job everyday. I'd speak to her every afternoon around the same time. She would be pulling this two-wheel cart on her way to the store.
When I saw her as we passed, I would say to her "good afternoon," or "have a nice day". She would reply with a

negative grumble or a negative "what's so good about today? and keep walking.

 This went on for about a year, until one day I was talking to a customer on that same street that I passed this little old lady on most everyday. I heard someone calling my name saying, "Hey, James aren't you going to tell me to have a nice day?" I looked up and it was that little old lady talking to me with a big smile on her face. She was going to the store with her cart, and I didn't see her pass me by because I was talking to a customer. I smiled back and I waved at her. I couldn't believe it; she even knew my name. After that day every time we passed each other, we spoke smiled and laughed. She later told me she had been going through some life changing events and that things were getting better. She also thanked me for speaking to her every day and being kind to her.

Now let's look at the other side of being nice and kind to others. If you are being nice and kind to others just to get a nice response back to make yourself, feel good, you are doing it for yourself. This is not coming from the heart, and you are not walking in love. Things could get ugly when you place two negative wires together. Just think if you responded back negatively to someone because they rejected your kindness and niceness. Number one, it makes you negative and rude as well. Number two, you have just set off the fourth of July and it's probably not the fourth of July you want to see.

Remember you don't know what's on that person's mind or what they are going through at that moment. What you say could cause them to snap and that little bit of negativity could take them over the edge. This could possibly bring harm to you or them out of anger. I would say, if you are not able to walk in love and not able to handle rejection of your kindness and niceness, it's better not to say anything to that person. You should be kind and nice to others and not expect anything back. It's not about us, it's about Jesus Christ walking in love. He was beat, spit upon, laughed at, talked about, and crucified and He still loved all those who did those bad things to Him, and He still asked God the Father to forgive them.

Then Jesus said, "Father, forgive them for they do not know what they do." And they divided his garments and cast lots. (Luke 23:34)

Remember:
* People aren't who they appear to be sometimes.
* We all have good and bad days.

* Don't take things personally.

* Don't wear your feelings on your sleeve.

* There are good and bad people.

* Everyone is not going to like you because you are kind or nice to them.

* Most importantly, we are all just ordinary people and not Jesus Christ. He's the only perfect one.

Chapter 4

Is nice being stupid?

Being nice to someone can mean a lot of things, but there are people who think that being nice to another human being is a sign of weakness and that you have the word "stupid "stamped on your forehead. They have no clue of how to accept a compliment, a friendly gesture, or someone doing something nice for them with no strings attached, because the environment that they are used to and the company they keep are the opposite of nice. They probably rarely have anyone that is nice to them.

You must be aware of some of the people who you are nice to because they will come at you from all sorts of angles. They will try to bully you, run games on you, steal from you, be mean to you, or lie to you because they associate nice as being a weakness and see you as a pushover. It is sort of like Satan in the bible walking around seeking whom he may devour.

Be self-controlled and alert. Your enemy the devil prowls around like a roaring lion looking for someone to devour. (1 Peter 5:8)

I remember when I first started my present job, I call it being tested. I had some of my peers at work trying to be mean to me because I was nice to everyone, and I tried to come to work in a good spirit everyday. I noticed some had bad attitudes towards me. I would ask them a question about the job, they would snap at me real fast and say go ask the supervisor or they would act like they didn't hear me and just ignore me. The work environment was not a good one for me at first. But as time past, I continued coming to work in a good spirit everyday and speaking to my co-workers and supervisors.

Things then started to change; I had a co-worker ask me one day "James how do you do it? "I said "do what?" The co-worker said "I never see you in a bad mood and you're always laughing and smiling. I said," it's God, I read my bible and I go to church every Sunday. I also said that the things in my last job that I had to do were far worse than this one and that this job is a lot easier. Pretty soon the nay sayers and some of the co-workers who had been mean to me at first started acting like human beings and those chips they had on their shoulders started to fall off. But I still had a couple of co-workers who were mean to me just out of spite and jealousy. They would talk bad about me to other co-workers and would go as far as telling the supervisor at work that I was disturbing them because I was laughing at work. When, in fact it, was about 5 or 6 of us co-workers laughing together and none of the others would get called back to the supervisor's office except me.

But, after I explained the situation, the supervisor would say that person is always complaining about something not to worry about anything and that I was one of their best employees, and to just stay away from him. About a couple of years passed and we got a new supervisor. That same person made the same complaint against me again. This time they brought that individual in and told him that he was the one with the problem and there was nothing wrong with me laughing at work and for him to stop complaining about nothing in so many words.

A few months later, that person who complained to management about me, He started speaking to me. The next thing I knew he was listening to scripture from the bible on his headset and was making comments to me about God and Jesus Christ on occasion. He also told me that if some days he didn't say anything to me not to take it personal, because he was going through some stuff at that time. I said, "no problem."

I had another encounter at my job with a customer. I crossed paths with every day while I was working out in the field. The customer would say "All you ever do is bring me bills."
They would be rude and say this in front of other people to embarrass me. But I still smiled and told the person to have a nice day. Some days I would respond back jokingly to the person. "If you pay your bills online and check that little block no paper copies you won't ever

have to see me again" or "stop yelling at me about your bills these are your bills not mine, if you don't want them stop making them". I guess I was kind of fed up, but anyway I felt bad saying that stuff to that person because after a while I started feeling that way inside. So, I stopped commenting back because I didn't want to feel that way, I was letting the devil win. So, I continued to be nice to the person even though the person continued being mean to me.

Then one day the retail person of the shop next door heard the person make that comment to me. "All you ever do is bring me bills". The person came over and said I'm tired of hearing you insult James all the time, he is nice to everybody, and we like him here on this street. After that day I had no more problems out of that person. I guess God sent one of his angels to rescue me that day. Well anyway to make a long story short, that person started speaking to me in a positive demeanor and today we have a positive relationship and have become friends and the person even told me that they were going through something in their life and is battling that problem today. Knowing what that person is going through in their everyday life I try to be more uplifting and in good spirit for that person every time I see them now. Because that person needs all the love, hope, and positive support they can get. That old saying is true about: When you think you have it bad, there is someone out there who has it worse than you. So, I would say continue to be nice to people, you don't have "stupid" stamped on your forehead. What you have stamped on your forehead is "unconditional love", the same love that Jesus has for each and everyone of us and he want's us to be nice to each other while we are here on earth.

Chapter 5

My secret to sustaining peace

There is no magic involved in one sustaining his or her peace. I try to look at the big picture and ask myself why is it important for me to sustain my peace? Number one, I keep my peace because I do not want to harbor anger, which brings hate to the heart. It's a bad feeling and I don't want to feel that way about anyone or anything. Number two when you're at peace you think better because you are calm. You make better decisions and good choices.

My most important reason for sustaining my peace is so that I can hear God. You cannot hear God if you are not at peace and there is a bunch of mess going on in your head all the time. When you are not at peace you hear evil, you think about things like getting revenge, jealousy, bad language, and some go as far as murder. There are plenty of jails occupied all over the world because someone lost their peace. God wants us to sustain our peace so we can hear him.

Turn from evil and do good; seek peace and pursue it. (Psalm 34:14)

Here are a few things that I have learned over the years that helped me sustain my peace:

* Be the bigger person.
* Learn to let things go.
* Don't always try to have the last word.
* Be nice to your enemies.
* Remain calm.
* Remember, it takes two to argue.

* It's not that serious.

* Some days are better than others.

* Pray for peace of mind.

This last one important. When you pray for peace of mind, avoid praying for the things of the world because they do not last forever. You see all these rich folks out there, they have everything-money, cars, houses, and all the worldly riches you can think of. But they still have no peace and are unhappy because they are looking in the wrong places. When you pursue the Word of God you will find peace. You will hear that still small voice. God's word is peace, and it lasts forever. It will last you a lifetime. Let's take the rich man in the Bible. He had everything, but he refused to give up the things of the world to inherit eternal life. He loved his possessions more; he could have had peace and everlasting life with Jesus.

Then Jesus looked around and said to His disciples, "How hard it is for those who have riches to enter the kingdom of God!" And the disciples were astonished at His words. But Jesus answered again and said to them, "Children how hard it is for those who trust in riches to enter the kingdom of God! "It is easier for a camel to go through the eye of a needle than for a rich man to enter the kingdom of God." (Mark 10:23-25)

Sustaining peace is a daily task and a daily fight for us all. You just don't wake up one morning and say," I'm cured, I have peace 24/7 now." You must seek peace and pursue it and make it part of your everyday life and know that we all are going to have trials and tribulations or our ups and downs of life. I know that what ever I'm going through, no matter what it is, God's word is the only thing that can bring me peace. If I have an anger issue, a death of a loved one, a financial need, or what ever the problem may be, I have my bible that I can reference God's word on what ever the issue might be and put God's word into action with prayer knowing at the end it will bring me peace and closure.

One last thing, it is ok to pray occasionally for a new car or a nice place to live or some of the other things in life, just make sure you are not idolizing these things and are not living above your means. As they say, don't try to keep up with the Joneses. If you are, being in debt is going to interrupt your peace. Keep God first and seek his word and you shall find peace

Chapter 6

Overcoming Issues with Family Members

When I say overcoming issues with family members, what is the first thing that comes to your mind? God help me? Who did what this time? or both. Let me also clarify family while you're marinating over that question. Your grandparents, father, mother, son, daughter, aunt, uncle, cousins, stepparents, brothers, and sisters. I think that covers most of family.

When it comes to family, it has got to be one of the hardest challenges in the world to overcome and walk in love and peace. It took me a long time to even put a dent in this area of my life. We all have family members that are good and bad. We love both the good and bad family members. But we hate the things that they do sometimes.

Your family members cause you more problems than your enemies do. Why? Think about it. You're not going to let your enemies get that close to you. But with your family members you tend to let your guard down. Your family members know how to press your buttons because of your love for them and the emotional ties you have with them. They know how to press your sympathy button, anger button, patience button, financial button, and many other buttons. Sometimes they press buttons that you never thought existed.

Dealing with family can be exhausting sometimes. Each family member has his or her own personality, their own needs and wants, pretty much their own everything. You must deal with each one differently. I would probably be somewhere in a psyche ward today or in some cave living as a hermit just wanting to get away from certain family members, if I hadn't... I have made great improvements in this area of my life and today I'm still working on it and making great progress. I have my love and peace for my family, but I still get those flare ups from certain family members at times. But now I know how to deal with them. How to put those fires out, maintain my love for them and keep my peace?

Now I'm going to answer that question. When I say overcoming issues with family members, what is the first thing that comes to my mind? God help me? Who did what this time? or both? My answer is God help me because I need the strength of God to help me. He is the only one that can help me in my opinion. God is my psychiatrist and my counselor, and it is all free of charge, no bills only a reward at the end if I succeed. God is my creator; your creator and he knows you better than anyone in the world. That includes yourself. Yes, he knows me better than I know me. It's like--you drive a Chevy. If it breaks down, you're not going to take it to a Ford dealer to get it repaired. You're going to take it to a Chevy dealer for repairs because they made the Chevy. They know the Chevy better than the Ford dealer because it's their product. They built it. Just like God built us human beings in His own image.

I must put God before my family, I love God more than my family. God is going to love me no matter what. God is not going to steal my love. God is not going to steal my peace. Just like God loved us more than his family, he let his son Jesus Christ die for our sins that we may have the opportunity for eternal life in heaven with him. He sacrificed his only son for us all.

"For God so loved the world that He gave His only begotten Son, that whoever believes in Him should not perish but have everlasting life. (John 3:16)

My family is second behind God. I don't think any of us could give up their son the way God did for a bunch of sinners. I would not want to be tested in this area by God. A lot of us would probably fail myself included. I believe that Abraham in the Bible in Genesis chapter twenty-two came closest to sacrificing his son Isaac for God.

When they reached the place, God had told him to go, Abraham built an altar there and arranged the wood on it. He bound his son Isaac and laid him on the altar, on top of the wood. Then he reached out his hand and took the knife to slay his son. But the angel of the Lord called out to him from heaven, "Abraham! Abraham!" "Here I am, "he replied. "Do not lay a hand on the boy," he said. "Do not do anything to him. Now I know that you fear God, because you have not withheld from me your son, your only son."

(Genesis 22:9-12 NIV)

Here are some things that I've learned to deal with when it comes to certain family members in maintaining my love for them and keeping my peace. The one thing you don't want to do with family members is turn your weapons on them. Meaning not real weapons, but the negative.

If you have a family member that is always pressing your financial button for a loan and never pays it back...

Learn from the past! Don't stress yourself out trying to get it back even if you really need that money. Keep your peace, because you already knew before you let them borrow it, they were not going to pay it back. Because they did it to you before and more than once. Just charge it up to the game and don't lend them anymore money. If you do give them more money, just give it to them don't make it a loan. You will be much happier and at peace.

If you have a family member who always waits until the last minute to do something and hands it off to you....

They usually make it sound so simple. "This is all you have to do for me, everything is taken care of." But at the same time, they forget to mention this one little thing. This totally throws all your plans for the day out of the window, puts you behind the eight ball and causes you all kind of anger, stress, and Lord knows what else. But you manage somehow to get it done and work yourself back to peace with the help of that still small voice the Holy Spirit. When you see that family member you ask them about the little thing they forgot to mention. They act like it was no big deal. At that moment you probably are wanting to snap, slap, hurt, choke, or even stab somebody. For this family member, learn how to say," No thank you." If you choose to help them, make sure your calendar is cleared for that day, you have nothing to do and are bored and need some excitement. Remember that anything could happen with this family member. Put on your bullet proof vest.

If you have a family member that needs a place to stay for a few weeks....

It's because their place is being repaired or it's been a year since they came to visit for the holiday and they're still living with you. This relative is my favorite. They're messy and don't clean up and expect someone else to do it. Your home now looks like a tsunami hit it and they have all these excuses. You get to the point where you are fed up and everybody start getting on everybody's nerves. Then you find yourself after work not really wanting to go home yet. When you do get home you're sitting in the driveway, in the car, listening to the radio tuned into a ministry station, having the word of God ministered to you before you go into the house. Saying to yourself:" Lord let me keep my peace and give me the words to say." And by that time your neighbor comes over to make sure you're okay because you've been sitting in your car for an extended period. They hear the gospel, see you in work attire relaxing. Politely they wave walking away not wanting to disturb you. Letting you unwind.

For this relative I would suggest that you get other family members to share in this responsibility. They are that person's family too. Don't take on the burden all by yourself.

These are just some of the things you must overcome with relatives to maintain your love for them and keep your peace. As I stated earlier, dealing with relatives is one of the hardest challenges you must overcome to keep your peace. Family members play on your emotions and emotional ties you have with them. Love God first, and more than your family, and stick to the word of God when it comes to family. It will put out those flare ups of anger, stress, irritation, or whatever it may be.

Pray this prayer, "God I 'm not my relatives' savior, You are. I'm handing them over to You. They are Your responsibility not mine, in Jesus' name I pray Amen." From that point on, you let God handle their problems. You continue to pray for them and leave it all to God. Now this prayer doesn't count for your children who are not adults, they are your responsibility and God gave them to you as a gift and expects you to raise them up in his word.

I just want to say this before I close. The subject of overcoming the issues of family members is a tough one to write about, without hurting anyone's feelings. You don't want to turn your weapons on your family. I want to thank God for all my family members. I love them all both good and bad. I especially want to thank Him for the good because they balance out the bad and give me hope and are examples for the family members that are challenging. I'm so thankful for the good, they never cause me problems. They are always loving and giving, always offering to help. I can count on them if needed, especially those who are walking in God's love and word. Bless you all.

Chapter 7

Count Your Blessings Not Your Problems

We all should be thankful for what we have and thank God for all the wonderful blessings that He has provided for us. Instead, to many times we take fore granted the things that we do have and feel that we are supposed to have these blessings automatically. We feel that someone owes us something and we should have more, when in fact we have more than enough, and no one owes us anything. Yes, I'm talking to you if you're reading this book, and especially you who live right here in the United States of America, where we are so blessed.

Here's an exercise. Take a blank piece of paper. Draw a line down the middle of it, at the top left write the word blessings. At the top right, write the word problems. I will bet everyone would have more blessings than problems, but don't do the exercise yet. First think about the word blessing and the word problems. Do you really know what they are? What are blessings? Blessings are things that God put in your life to make it better. They are positive. What are problems? Problems are things essential in your life. They are negative and we do our best to overcome them. Some of them, if not overcome could mean life or death.

Instead of characterizing our blessings and problems as such we put them in the category of have and have-nots, as in: I have this, that's a blessing. And I don't have this, that's a problem. Pretty much our want and needs list. We lose the real understanding and true meaning of what a blessing or a problem really is. We lose the appreciation of a blessing that God has given us. We get an attitude at the world because things aren't going right in a certain area of our life, and we label it as a problem when it's not.

I wish just for a week we could all trade places with someone in one of those third world countries where the people are dying of hunger, thirst, curable disease and where the life expectancy of a child is five years old. Some of you right now are saying that's their problem over there. No, it's the worlds problem. You are blessed not to be born in one of those places. If you were born in one of those places, would the words "their problem" even be coming out of your mouth? I think not. So, make sure you write this down as your first blessing on your blank piece of paper: I live in the United States of America.

For some of you who have been sheltered all your life I would give a day. A week might be a bit too much for you in one of those third world countries. You would probably need professional help of some sort to get over the shock after a week trying to understand what you just experienced over there. The light bulb would then come on and your brain would start registering again what's really a blessing and what's really a problem.

Can you picture yourself getting up in the morning not going to your job, but instead your new job is looking for clean water to drink? Would you say this is a problem or a blessing? Most of us eat breakfast, lunch, and dinner daily with a midnight snack. How would you feel if the only thing you ate for the week was half of a sandwich that you found in the dumpster while looking for food? Would you say this is a blessing or a problem? These are what you call real problems, dying from hunger and thirst are not blessings, but having clean disease-free water and three meals a day with a midnight snack are clearly blessings that we take for granted. We look at our blessings as something that is normal for us. But should be thanking God on the daily for them. Everything that is positive that happens to us and everything positive that we have are blessings from God.

Every good gift and every perfect gift is from above, and comes down from the Father of lights, with whom there is no variation or shadow of turning. (James 1:17)

Now that we have covered blessings and problems and you have truly and honestly thought about them, you can jot them down on your blank piece of paper. You will no doubt be thanking God for all the wonderful blessings you have in your life, if you can manage to fit them all on that blank piece of paper. Always count your blessings, not your problems. You have far more blessings than problems. Remember this when you think you have it bad. There is someone out there who has it worse, and what you call a problem may just be a want. We in the United States of America are *too blessed to be stressed.*

Chapter 8

Live Your Life Like There Is No Tomorrow

If you knew today would be your last day here on earth? Would you be sad? Would you be worried? Would you have fun? Would you spend it with your loved ones and close friends? What would you do?

I know that's a tough one to sink your teeth into. I would say this: we all know that one day we are going to leave here with a one-way ticket to either heaven or hell. Me personally, I prefer heaven, but that's not up to me or you, it's up to God. I would not want to know when my last day on earth is. I can enjoy the life God has given me here on earth by not knowing. I can enjoy it with peace like he wants me to. Tomorrow isn't promised to me. For this reason, I say live your life like there is no tomorrow because there maybe no tomorrow.

Do not boast about tomorrow, for you do not know what a day may bring forth.

(Proverbs 27:1)

As I get older, I try more and more to live my life like there is not tomorrow. I find myself getting closer and closer to God. Certain things don't matter anymore. It's not that I don't care, but I must look at the big picture. Which is, I could be gone tomorrow or even today. The same issues, and task of everyday life, will still be here the next day after I'm gone for someone else to deal with.

Another thing don't let fear stop you from living your life. You only get one life in the flesh. Do things that make you happy, spend time with loved ones, have fun, laugh, smile, worry less, hand all your problems over to God. Most importantly, spend as much time with God as possible. Do your best to be obedient in his word and hope that you have eternal life with Him in heaven when you leave earth.

While you're living your life like there's no tomorrow don't make plans. Just live. Everyday you wake up and breath and have life in your body, you thank God and live it like its your last. If you must make plans, for example, let God know that you are planning a trip to Europe or Hawaii next summer. That way you are not boasting, a thing which God dislikes. We make plans through our mind and heart. God directs our footsteps; He has the final say so in all our lives. Our God is a jealous God. He gives life, we do not. You shouldn't make these types of plans unless you go through him.

It's like asking for permission to go on a field trip next summer to Europe or Hawaii. I know we all remember when we were in school and for us to go on that field trip with our school, we had to get a signed permission slip from our parents to go. The same thing with God our Father you need a permission slip. To get that permission slip from God you need to ask Him to bless you with that trip to Europe or Hawaii next summer. God can hear you and won't consider you boasting which He dislikes. In the book of James in the bible it talks about boasting.

"Come now, you who say, "Today or tomorrow we will go to such and such city, spend a year there, buy and sell, and make a profit", whereas you do not know what will happen tomorrow. For what is your life? It is even a vapor that appears for a little time and then vanishes away. Instead, you ought to say, "If the lord wills we shall live and do this or that." But now you boast in your arrogance. All such boasting is evil. Therefore, to him who knows to do good and does not do it, to him it is sin." (James 4:13-17)

Letting God know that you want to go on that trip next summer, maybe one of the smartest things you've ever done in your life. You maybe prolonging your life. My grandmother lived to be 100 years old. I remember her always praying and speaking to God; seeking His blessing in advance before she did things. God is our creator He will be here when we are gone. Be happy enjoy every breath that you take and every beautiful thing that God has created for us to enjoy here on earth.

One last thing don't be a fool when enjoying life, there is a place designed for fools and it's called the bottomless pit. Be obedient to God and avoid the ungodly things of the world. God loves you and want's you to be happy and enjoy life.

Chapter 9

Smile and Laugh as Much as Possible

What makes you laugh? What makes you smile? Who makes you smile? Who makes you laugh? Is it ok to laugh? Is it ok to smile?

No matter what your answer is to these questions there's no wrong answer. We all smile and laugh some more than others; even unhappy people laugh and smile sometimes. I try to smile and laugh everyday because it keeps me happy, and it just makes everyday life easier to deal with. I can't see myself walking around all day long with that stupid monster face on, looking at people and not smiling or saying anything.

That gives off bad vibes. Believe it or not, if people get to know you like that they put up walls against you. They might be scared, suspicious, overly cautious, and are defensive, especially if they don't know you.

Knowing God makes me smile, knowing that I have access to him 24/7 and that he loves me no matter what. I start my day off with God every morning. After I spend time with him my day starts with a smile. I go to my job and certain people make me smile and laugh because I'm glad to see them. The same with my customers. Some make me laugh and smile because I'm glad to see them. Some of the things that my friends at work do and my friends in the community do make me laugh and smile too. Do you know when you laugh it brings a smile to your face it's called laughter. God wants us to laugh and smile. In the book of

Proverbs, it talks about a happy heart and a cheerful face.

A happy heart makes the face cheerful, but heartache crushes the spirit.

(Proverbs 15:13 NIV)

Here are some gifts from God of smiles and laughter that I enjoy on the daily.

I walk by this house every day and sometimes I hear one of my customers singing. I hear music in the background. When I hear that customer singing, it puts a smile on my face, and I laugh on the inside. They sound happy and are really feeling the music. When I see them, I'll say "I heard you in there cutting that record. We "gonna" have to get you a deal with a record label." Then we laugh, smile and joke about it.

I have a couple of friends on the job we exchange jokes on the daily. We try to make our place of work a better work environment. Some are funny, some are not. But we manage somehow to turn the bad jokes into laughter as well. When we get some good ones, others at work laugh along with us. Sometimes it creates a great work environment when you get others at work smiling and laughing. Instead of a bunch of grumpy people always mad about something. Sometimes the supervisor laughs and smiles at our ridiculous jokes to.

Do you know you can laugh on the inside? When you are thinking about something, it could be a childhood memory. But where you are now you can't laugh out loud because it would be disruptive to others. It's like being at the opera. You are enjoying the show. You have a smile on your face, but you dare not laugh out loud or you could find yourself being escorted to the nearest exit.

Have you ever been caught daydreaming with a smile on your face by someone and they say to you "What's so funny?" You look at them with this big grin on your face and reply "Nothing. I was just thinking about something." You really want to laugh out loud, but you don't because you don't want them to think you are laughing at them. The kindest response then is to tell them what you were thinking about and let them share in your happiness.

Don't let people steal your joy because you laugh and smile. That is your gift from God. He wants you to smile and laugh and be happy. There will be others who are unhappy and always miserable because of certain things in their lives. They haven't learned how to be happy, to smile, and laugh. They may even have negative comments towards you just because you are happy. But don't let that bother you. Continue the righteous path of smiling and laughter. In the book of Psalms, it talks about God laughing at the wicked.

The wicked plots against the just, And gnashes at him with his teeth. The Lord laughs at him, For He sees that his day is coming. The wicked have drawn the sword and have bent their bow, to cast down the poor and the needy, to slay those who are of upright conduct. Their sword shall enter their own heart, and their bows shall be broken

(Psalm 37:12-15)

I love my pastor at the church I attend. He is always full of energy, and he smiles and laughs a lot. It's also contagious throughout our church. We all laugh and smile a lot in church. One of his favorite things to say is "church was never meant to be boring." I say amen to that pastor."

I love my family they make me smile and laugh. When I think about the memories over the years, it puts a smile on my face. Even the not so good moments bring laughter to my heart. I thank God for blessing me with my family and keeping me grounded. For teaching me how to laugh and smile and be happy. In Jesus name, I pray amen.

Chapter 10

Miracles Bring Joy

Miracles come from the power of God. They bring us joy, happiness, and peace. In the bible we read about the miracles that God performed and the miracles that Jesus performed. Some of us know that miracles are real, we know people that have received miracles from God.

I have a friend who had a tumor the size of a cantaloupe removed. My friend and his family went through a lot of physicians over the years to perform a particular surgery to remove the tumor. The physicians they saw previously would not perform this surgery to remove the tumor, because they feared it would be unsuccessful. But my friend and his family kept praying to God for that miracle until one-day God brought them the right physician that would perform the surgery. The surgery was performed by the physician, there were no complication's, the tumor was successfully removed and there was no cancer found. Today my friend is walking on their own and there is no doubt this was a miracle from the highest.

Imagine all the stress and worry my friend and their family endured over the years dealing with his medical condition and the numerous physician visits. That miracle brought my friend and their family joy, peace, and happiness. It took away their worry, stress, and pain. They had the faith to keep believing in God and for a miracle. It makes me think about the lady in the bible with the blood flow problem for twelve years and she spent all her money on physicians and her condition got worse instead of better. But she believed and had faith in a miracle. If she could just touch Jesus she would be healed.

And suddenly, a woman who had a flow of blood for twelve years came from behind and touched the hem of his garment. For she said to herself, "If only I may touch his garment, I shall be made well." But Jesus turned around, and when he saw her, He said, "Be of good cheer, daughter; your faith has made you well." And the woman was made well from that hour.
(Matthew 9:20-22)

I want to share another miracle; this one involves the pastor of a church. He suffered an aneurism while preaching at church. He had a blood vessel hemorrhaging in his brain and the doctors couldn't stop the bleeding. The doctors didn't think he would make it through the night. But some how through the prayers of the congregation and that pastor's faith, God healed the pastor, and he has recovered from the aneurism. He is back preaching and teaching the gospel stronger than before. The church is a happier church full of joy after God brought them this incredible miracle. I'll bet those doctors know who the real physician is, they call him doctor Jesus.

The last miracle I want to share with you is about another friend of mine. There was a problem with their internal organs. Let's just say they needed two healthy organs. I was able to witness the power of one of God's many miracles. My friend was blessed with new organs, and I remember seeing my friend for the first time after my friend received the miracle from God. It was like looking at a new person, it wasn't that my friend's appearance changed. It's kind of hard to explain but when I looked into my friend's eyes it was like looking at a different person. It was my friend, but it was like someone had breathed life into my friend's body. You could see that the spirit of God was inside my friend. Where before my friend received the miracle from God you saw the opposite. He looked weary and sounded tired all the time. I believe my friend's faith in God made my friend well just like in the book of Matthew with the little old lady. My friend never complained, never felt sorry, was always positive, and believed that God would heal the condition.

In the Bible, miracles were referred to as signs and wonders also. When Jesus walked the earth people wanted to see proof that God was for real. They wanted Jesus to give them a sign, a wonder, or a miracle. But Jesus refused to do it for that reason. When Jesus did perform miraculous acts, he did them to let everybody know that he was the son of God and whoever believed in him would have eternal life in heaven with him.

And truly Jesus did many other signs in the presence of His disciples, which are not written in this book; but these are written that you may believe that Jesus is the Christ, the Son of God, and that believing you may have life in His name.

(John 20:30-31)

I thank God for letting me be a witness to his power and giving me the understanding of a miracle. It is truly a blessing to know what the power of God can do if you have faith in him and believe in him with all your heart and all your might.

Chapter 11

Do You Believe in Angels?

Most of us know that angels are real from reading the bible. If someone said to you, describe an angel. The first thing that would come to a lot of minds would be this man or woman- like person with wings and a halo over the top of their head. But we all know that is a fairy tale description of an angel.

Did you know that the bible say's in Psalm 148 verses 2 and 5 angels were created by God but does not specify in what image? It says that God created us in his image. The bible say's that angels are spirits.

But to which of the angels has He ever said: "Sit at My right hand, till I make your enemies your footstool?" Are they not all ministering spirits sent forth to minister for those who will inherit salvation? (Hebrews 1:13-14)

There are good angels and bad angels. The good angels do God's work they are obedient to Him. They serve Him and help protect us. They are also messengers and bearers of good news. The bad angels are our enemies and Satan is the number one bad angel. He would be considered like the FBI's most dangerous criminal here in the United States. Satan and his angels are deceivers, liars, and bad spirits here on earth. I truly believe there are good angels here on earth protecting us from the bad spirits.

I can remember years ago when I was in my mid-twenties, I had just come home from hanging out with some of my Army buds at work. I did have some wine when I was out with the fellas. My wife and son were gone for the weekend, visiting her parents and I was home alone. When I got home, I turned on the tv in the bedroom and went into the kitchen. I was hungry so I put two hot dogs in a pot on the stove and turned it on. Then I went back to the bedroom and set on the end of the bed and took my shoes off. That is the last thing I remember.

The next thing I knew it was morning, I had passed out on the bed. I could hear the birds singing at my window. When I woke up and finally remembered the pot I'd left on the stove, it scared me. I didn't smell any smoke and when I went into the kitchen the pot was still on the stove. The stove dial was still in the on position. The stove isle that the pot was sitting on had burnt out, there was still some water in the pot. I said "thank you, God" to myself. This could have been bad. Number one I thanked God that I didn't die from smoke inhalation and the house didn't burn down with me in it. Number two, I thank God for electric stoves back then. If it had been a gas stove, there would not have been an isle burned out. I would have died from smoke inhalation and would have been burned up in the fire with the house. Number three, my family would have been devastated had I died that night. My wife a widow, my son fatherless, and my mom and siblings heart broken.

The only thing I could think of was God having sent one of his angels to protect me and keep me safe from the bad spirit I had consumed. There could be no other answer for this. I still think about that night today even though it has been over 25 years. I tell myself through the grace of God I'm still here today. Knowing that I shouldn't be here. I still get scared when I think about it.

I'm somewhat scared right now as I share this with you. There's no doubt in my mind that I was saved by an angel. It's sort of like in the book of Psalm. God must have seen something good in me and had mercy on me that night.

No evil shall befall you, nor shall any plaque come near your dwelling; For He shall give His angels charge over you, to keep you in all your ways. In their hands they shall bear you up, lest you dash your foot against a stone. (Psalm 91:10-12)

I also believe that we all have encountered good angels here on earth and have not known it. In the bible it talks about angels appearing in the form of men. All those people we encounter on the daily that may look homeless or homely in appearance could be angels. Just take one minute to think about it. How many times have you run across somebody like this? You notice something different about their demeanor, they speak rather meekly and kindly. They may ask for money for food or just simply strike up a conversation. But we are rude to them because of the way they are dressed and smell. We assume they are no good, they're thieves, drug addicts, or worse. You could be getting tested by God.

You are supposed to help the poor and treat everyone the same regardless of who they are and what they look like. They are human beings just like you and me. If they are hungry, give them something to eat. If you have the time, just talk with them. They get lonely too, just like you and me.

There was one morning that I was on my way to work I stopped to mail a letter at the post office. There was this homeless man in the lobby sitting down. He asked me if I could spare a little change for some coffee. I think I gave him a dollar; I had fixed me a sack lunch to take to work and I really wanted to eat my lunch that day. But something kept saying to me when I was leaving the lobby: give the homeless man your lunch. When I got in my truck to drive off that still small voice I heard again. This time it said what did I tell you. Give him your lunch. So, I got out of my vehicle and gave him my lunch. As soon as I gave it to him, the homeless man started eating it and thanked me. He was very happy and gracious, and I drove off.

I got to thinking what just happened. I know that was the Holy Spirit talking to me because I've had that experience before of the holy spirit talking to me. Then I thought could that have been an angel too, or just the Holy Spirit. Which ever one it was I think I did what God wanted me to do that day and at that moment. The book of Hebrews talks about entertaining angels.

Do not forget to entertain strangers, for by so doing some have unwittingly entertained angels.

    (Hebrews 13:2)

I'm very happy to know that there are good angels here on earth. They are good spirits, and they protect us from the bad spirits. Even though we really don't know who they are I thank God for angels and sending one to save my life.

Chapter 12

Love Like Jesus Loves

If we could all love one another like Jesus loves each one of us, the world would be a better place.

There would be no arguments, no one getting angry, no one stressed out, no worry, no crimes, no murder. It probably wouldn't be too far from being in Heaven. I've never been to heaven, but I have a good imagination and the book of Revelation is my favorite biblical book. Those who have never read the book of Revelation, its the last book of the bible. It talks about Jesus coming back and it talks about what Heaven is going to be like when we get there if we are fortunate to make it. We won't have to worry about anything.

"And God will wipe away every tear from their eyes, there will be no more death, nor sorrow, nor crying. There shall be no more pain, for the former things have passed away." (Revelation 21:4)

Jesus love for us is unconditional. He even loved us through suffering. Here's what I mean by suffering love:

you must love people who are your enemies, people who do stuff to you. You must love even if you don't want to. You must put up with difficult behavior from people and overlook it. I'm not talking about overlooking something that is breaking the law. I'm talking about the way people act, their demeanor, their behavior, their attitude, the crazy stuff they do. Jesus still loved us through his suffering on the cross when he was beaten and crucified. He still loved us through his suffering and pain. There's no way I could have done that.

Don't be selfish when you can help someone. That's not walking in love or loving like Jesus loved. Jesus was patient with people and gave his time to help others. Giving up your time to help someone even if you don't want too is loving like Jesus.

People can really get on your nerves sometimes. But still have patience like Jesus and be loving and kind to others. Decide to help others and try to make someone's life better everyday. I know when loving like Jesus loves, you feel like a person being used sometimes. I know that's how I feel sometimes. But I know that through all the suffering love, I'm a representative and servant of Jesus Christ and I want people to know that is how Jesus loved to the very end. It's not about me, it's about him. In the book of John chapter 13 Jesus spoke to the disciples about loving one another right before he was crucified.

"A new commandment I give to you, that you love one another; as I have loved you, that you also love one another. "By this all will know that you are My disciples, if you have love for one another." (John 13:34-35)

Loving like Jesus loves keeps you at peace. It keeps you cheerful. It keeps you happy. And it keeps that unconditional love for others in your heart. People can see the love of Jesus in you, and I believe that is what Jesus wanted us and others to know when he said we are known by our fruit.

You don't have to take on the world's problems. When I say to help others and try to make someone's life better everyday. I'm talking about small and simple things:

* Mailing a letter for a friend,
* Giving a friend a ride to work.
* Picking up something from the store for a spouse or friend
* Spending 5 or 10 minutes just being a listener to a lonely senior citizen.

Little things like this can make a world of difference to people. It can make a difference between their day being a pleasant one instead of a tired, sad, lonely, or stressed-out day.

God wants us all to be happy every day. Let's start by loving each other like Jesus loves us.

Book Acknowledgements

I would first like to thank and praise God the Father. For giving me the ability and the wisdom to write this book. The goal of "Daily Wisdom" is to help people deal with everyday life, to be happy, cheerful, at peace, and to love each other.

I would also like to thank Sharon Stevens; she was the vessel that God used to give me the assignment to write "Daily Wisdom." I want to thank the Reverend Patrick Crerar, Mr. Craig Strickland, Ms. Rosalie Love, and Mr. Lawrence Tiberi for all their feedback and positive support.

I want to thank all the great men and women of God out there that have affected me in a positive way in my journey to love like Jesus loves. I truly thank each and everyone of them.

To all the readers out there, I thank you for supporting "Daily Wisdom." I hope it helps you find peace, love, happiness, and wisdom in your everyday life. God has given each and everyone of you a talent. What ever your talent is use it for the kingdom of God.

I thank everyone that was involved in the creation of this book. God Bless you all, In Jesus mighty name I pray, "Amen".

Made in the USA
Columbia, SC
13 February 2023